P-40 TOMAHAWK AND KITTYHAWK

In RAF Service - Europe and North Africa

NEIL ROBINSON

DEVELOPMENT XP-40

Inset: Where it all started... The XP-40 prototype was allocated the US Army Air Corps serial 38-010, when it started life as the tenth production P-36A. Although the cockpit remained in the same position and the rear fuselage configuration was the same as the P-36/Hawk 75 series, when it was fitted with a 12-cylinder Allison V-1710-19 in-line engine it added nearly three feet to the nose. Note the original position of the radiators for the liquid cooled engine in a scoop under the fuselage (arrowed).

Main photo: When the powerplant was changed to the 1,100hp V-1710-33, the radiators were moved to under the nose, apparently for fear they might be damaged by debris thrown up by the slipstream on take-off and landing. Note the barrels of the two .50 inch calibre machine guns over the cowling. The wing-under surfaces carried the US ARMY markings.

After the design was further refined and modified, in April 1939 the US Army ordered 524 P-40-CUs, as the type was now known, powered by a 1,090hp Allison V-1710-33 engine. The overall design of the nose section had been simplified and streamlined; the fairing under the nose, for two coolant radiators and an oil cooler radiator, was enlarged and moved further forward, with cooling flaps at the rear, and a central scoop was added on the top of the cowling as a carburettor intake. No wing armament had been fitted at this stage. The aircraft was in overall natural metal finish with USAAC white star in a blue disc with red centre national markings above and below both wings. A blue vertical bar with thirteen red and white horizontal bars appeared on the rudder.

Below: The first flight of a production P-40-CU took place in April 1940, and deliveries to the USAAC started in the June. 199 P-40-CUs were delivered before the remainder of the order was completed as P-40Bs and P-40Cs. Important improvements included the introduction of flush riveting (that reduced drag); and the P-36-style main undercarriage covers replaced with two smaller doors that only covered the u/c leg when the gear was retracted. Individual exhaust manifolds for each cylinder were fitted as standard to replace the single exhaust manifold either side.

Left: The Armée de l'Air were originally to be the first overseas customer for the P-40, an order for 230 Hawk 81As, (the export designation of the P-40-CU), being placed in October 1939. The aircraft never reached their intended customer due to the fall of France in June 1940. The British Purchasing Commission took the opportunity to acquire the aircraft, receiving some 140 airframes that were designated Tomahawk Mk I.

This photo is thought to be a doctored image with a spurious airbrushed camouflage finish representing a French Armée de l'Air scheme.

Tomahawk Mk I (Hawk 81A-1) and Tomahawk Mk II (Hawk 81A-2)

Tomahawk Mk I, (Hawk 81A-1) AH762 – from the ex-Armée de l'Air order – was one of 140 airframes that still had French instrumentation, and lacked armour, self-sealing fuel tanks and bullet-proof windscreens. Camouflaged in American equivalent shades of Dark Earth and Dark Green upper surfaces with Sky (or American Sky Gray) under surfaces, the national markings were applied in decal form. Of note is the Dark Earth spinner and the large non-standard fin flash. The 'stepped' pitot tube (arrowed) on the port wing was fitted to all British-operated Tomahawks and early Kittyhawks.

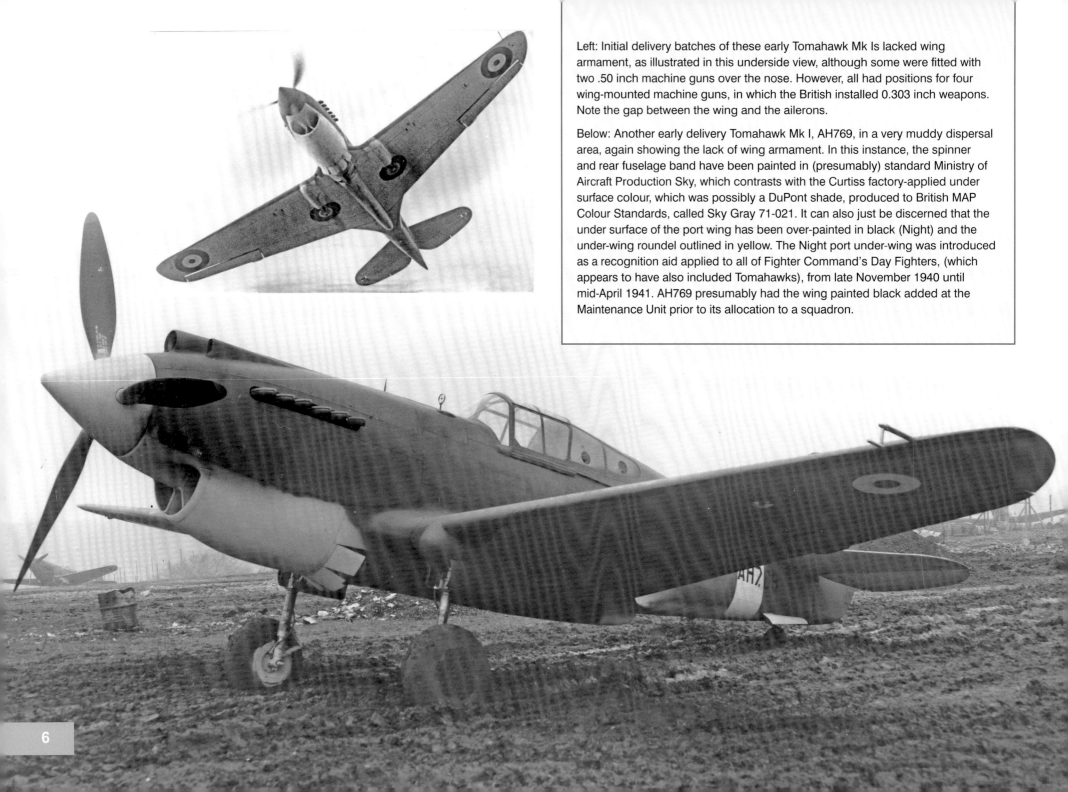

Left: Initial delivery batches of these early Tomahawk Mk Is lacked wing armament, as illustrated in this underside view, although some were fitted with two .50 inch machine guns over the nose. However, all had positions for four wing-mounted machine guns, in which the British installed 0.303 inch weapons. Note the gap between the wing and the ailerons.

Below: Another early delivery Tomahawk Mk I, AH769, in a very muddy dispersal area, again showing the lack of wing armament. In this instance, the spinner and rear fuselage band have been painted in (presumably) standard Ministry of Aircraft Production Sky, which contrasts with the Curtiss factory-applied under surface colour, which was possibly a DuPont shade, produced to British MAP Colour Standards, called Sky Gray 71-021. It can also just be discerned that the under surface of the port wing has been over-painted in black (Night) and the under-wing roundel outlined in yellow. The Night port under-wing was introduced as a recognition aid applied to all of Fighter Command's Day Fighters, (which appears to have also included Tomahawks), from late November 1940 until mid-April 1941. AH769 presumably had the wing painted black added at the Maintenance Unit prior to its allocation to a squadron.

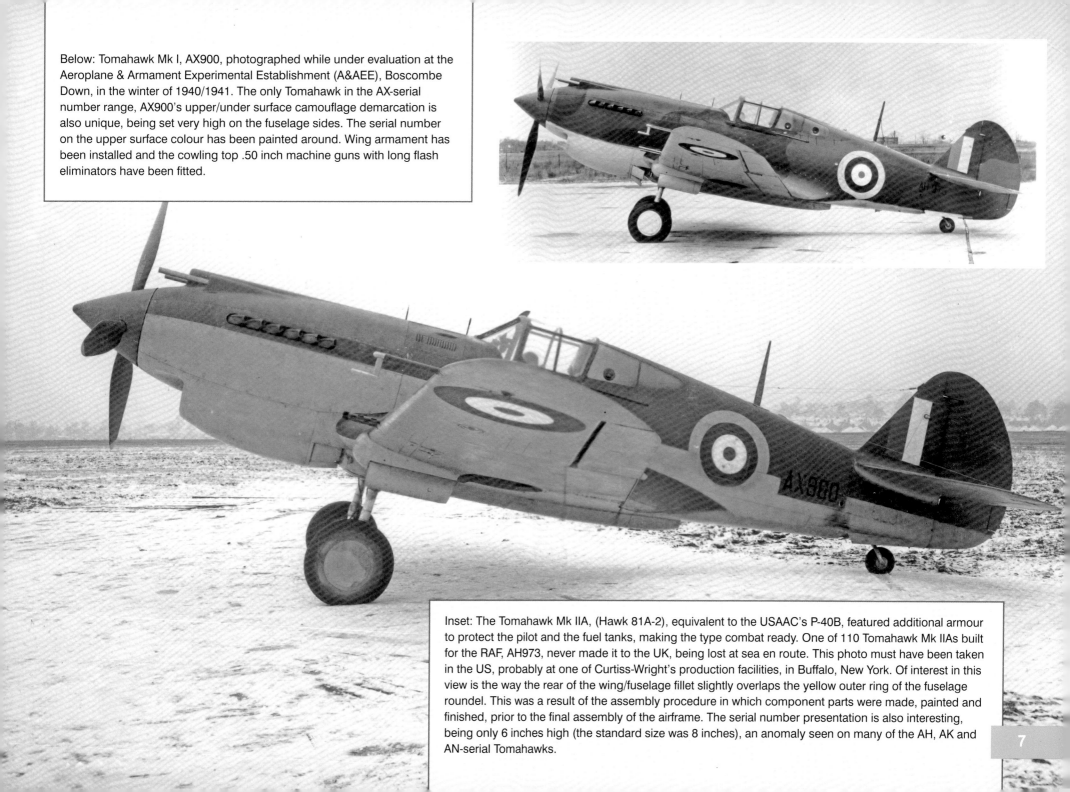

Below: Tomahawk Mk I, AX900, photographed while under evaluation at the Aeroplane & Armament Experimental Establishment (A&AEE), Boscombe Down, in the winter of 1940/1941. The only Tomahawk in the AX-serial number range, AX900's upper/under surface camouflage demarcation is also unique, being set very high on the fuselage sides. The serial number on the upper surface colour has been painted around. Wing armament has been installed and the cowling top .50 inch machine guns with long flash eliminators have been fitted.

Inset: The Tomahawk Mk IIA, (Hawk 81A-2), equivalent to the USAAC's P-40B, featured additional armour to protect the pilot and the fuel tanks, making the type combat ready. One of 110 Tomahawk Mk IIAs built for the RAF, AH973, never made it to the UK, being lost at sea en route. This photo must have been taken in the US, probably at one of Curtiss-Wright's production facilities, in Buffalo, New York. Of interest in this view is the way the rear of the wing/fuselage fillet slightly overlaps the yellow outer ring of the fuselage roundel. This was a result of the assembly procedure in which component parts were made, painted and finished, prior to the final assembly of the airframe. The serial number presentation is also interesting, being only 6 inches high (the standard size was 8 inches), an anomaly seen on many of the AH, AK and AN-serial Tomahawks.

Another Tomahawk Mk IIA from the same batch as AH973, AH925 shows several differences, including positioning of the fuselage roundel and size of the serial number, this time applied in the standard 8 inches high. Other interesting differences include the application of MAP Sky paint to the propeller spinner and the rear fuselage band, which may have been when the serial number was re-applied at the correct size. AH925 was another airframe that didn't see front-line service (which was maybe the reason it was devoid of armament) and spent it service life with the Central Flying School (CFS), A&AEE, and 30 Operational Training Unit (OTU), before being Struck off Charge (SoC) in December 1944.

The distinctive P-40 scalloped and glazed rear cockpit area behind the pilot was an attempt to improve rearward visibility without having to open the canopy.

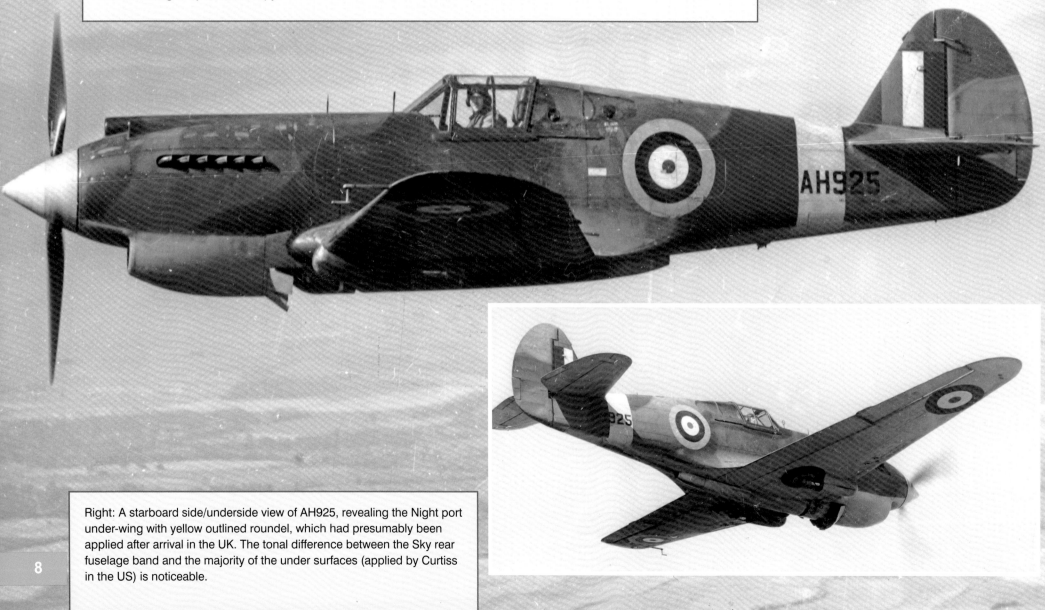

Right: A starboard side/underside view of AH925, revealing the Night port under-wing with yellow outlined roundel, which had presumably been applied after arrival in the UK. The tonal difference between the Sky rear fuselage band and the majority of the under surfaces (applied by Curtiss in the US) is noticeable.

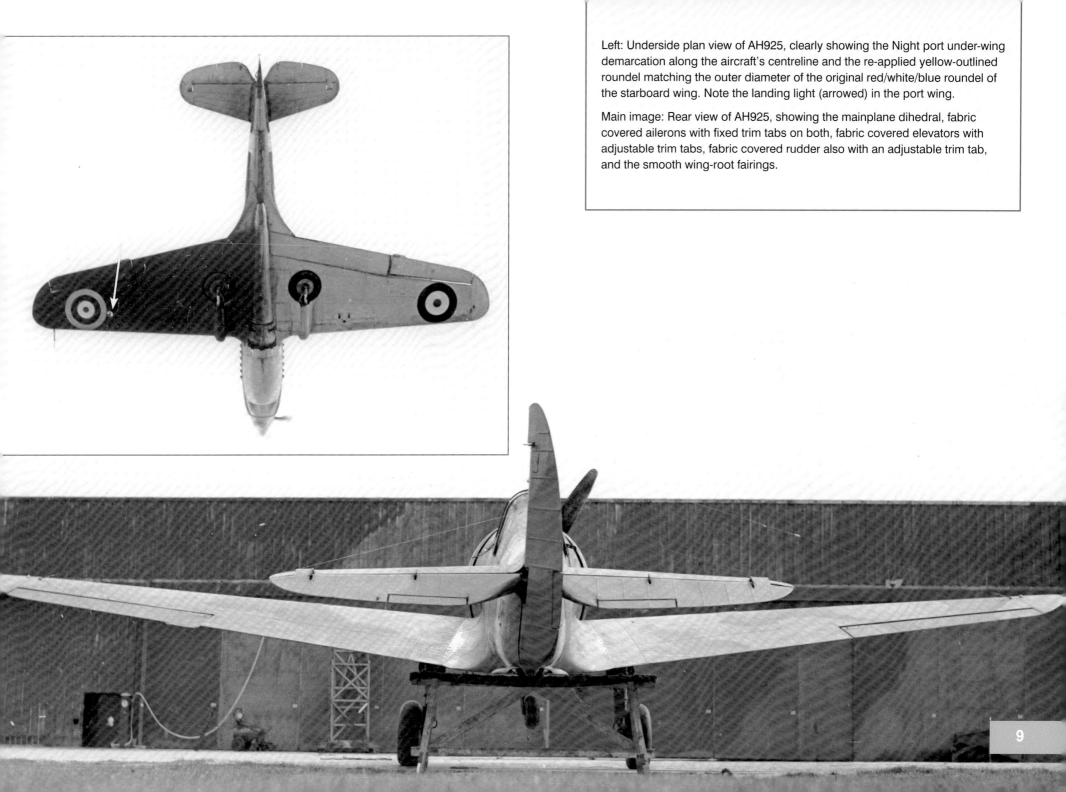

Left: Underside plan view of AH925, clearly showing the Night port under-wing demarcation along the aircraft's centreline and the re-applied yellow-outlined roundel matching the outer diameter of the original red/white/blue roundel of the starboard wing. Note the landing light (arrowed) in the port wing.

Main image: Rear view of AH925, showing the mainplane dihedral, fabric covered ailerons with fixed trim tabs on both, fabric covered elevators with adjustable trim tabs, fabric covered rudder also with an adjustable trim tab, and the smooth wing-root fairings.

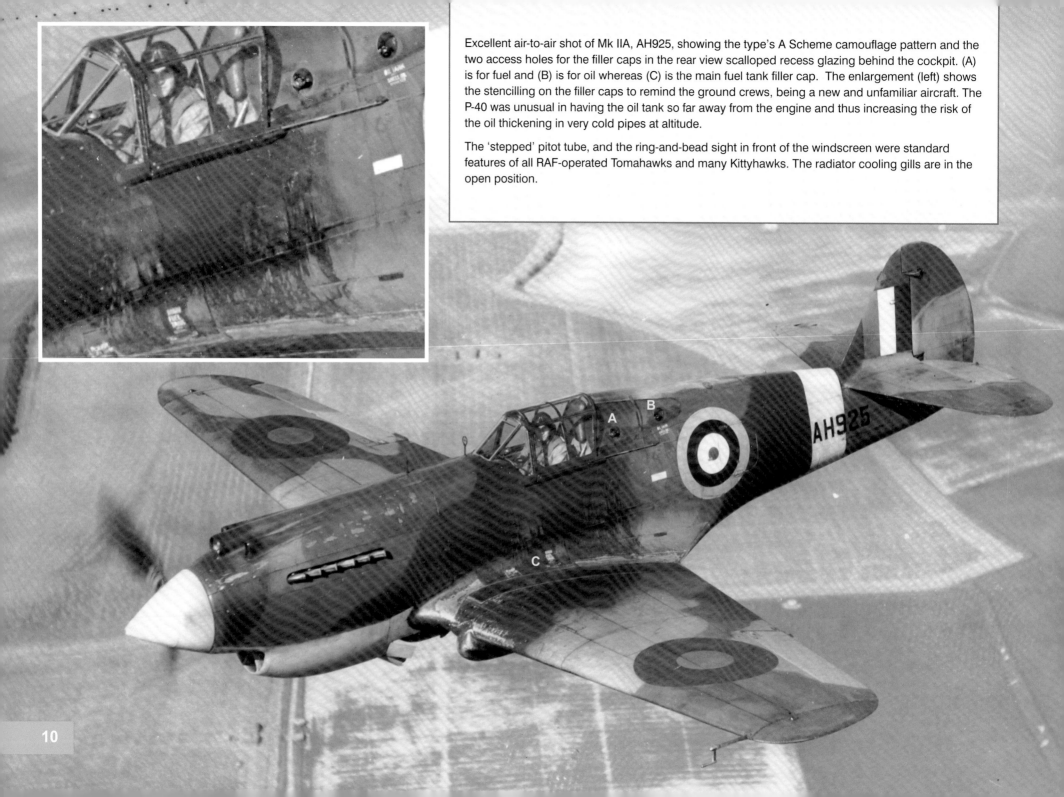

Excellent air-to-air shot of Mk IIA, AH925, showing the type's A Scheme camouflage pattern and the two access holes for the filler caps in the rear view scalloped recess glazing behind the cockpit. (A) is for fuel and (B) is for oil whereas (C) is the main fuel tank filler cap. The enlargement (left) shows the stencilling on the filler caps to remind the ground crews, being a new and unfamiliar aircraft. The P-40 was unusual in having the oil tank so far away from the engine and thus increasing the risk of the oil thickening in very cold pipes at altitude.

The 'stepped' pitot tube, and the ring-and-bead sight in front of the windscreen were standard features of all RAF-operated Tomahawks and many Kittyhawks. The radiator cooling gills are in the open position.

Right: One of the relatively few Tomahawk Mk IIBs to be used operationally in the UK, AK162, SY•N of 613 Squadron, photographed flying out of RAF Andover, Hampshire, in the summer of 1941, not long after delivery. The Tomahawks were used alongside the squadron's Lysanders, operating both types in radar calibration and Army Co-operation Exercise roles, until replaced by North American Mustang Mk Is in June 1942.

Below: An unidentified early delivery Tomahawk Mk II, probably a Mk IIA, photographed in a scenic dispersal area in the summer of 1941. The aircraft has the MAP Sky spinner and rear fuselage band applied and appears to have a black (Night) port under wing, with matching port mainwheel hub. Note the extensive stencilling on the propeller blade.

Left: Mk IIA, AH892 RM•D banking to reveal the area of Night under the port wing and the large individual aircraft letter 'D' under the starboard wing, which were applied as a special tactical exercise marking. The code letter under the nose appears to be 'M' – perhaps its previous code letter.

Right: Mk I AH791 RM•E also has a Night port wing underside with yellow-outlined roundel and large individual code letter 'E' under the starboard wing, whereas Mk IIA AH896 RM•Y appears to just have plain Sky/Sky Gray under-surfaces.

Main image: This trio of 26 Squadron Tomahawks was probably photographed on a training flight in June/July 1941. Based at RAF Gatwick, Sussex, at the time. The photo shows Mk IIAs AH893 RM•D and AH896 RM•Y with Mk I AH791 RM•E, (note the lack of fuselage aerial mast on AH791). As 26 Squadron's Tomahawks operated in the low-level tactical reconnaissance role, they were fitted with oblique camera ports on the port fuselage side – the camera port hatch on AH893 RM•D possibly coming from another aircraft as it has no yellow outline to the section of roundel on it. This shot also shows the difference between the A Scheme on RM•D and RM•E, and the B Scheme on RM•Y. RM•E and RM•Y have the squadron's 'Springbok's head' on the white section of the fin flash.

Below left: Another shot of Mk IIA, AH896 RM•Y, this time showing the upper surfaces. The port wing appears to have been repainted and the port red/blue roundel has a different size centre to the one on the starboard wing. After a period of training, in October 1941 the squadron's Tomahawks began to fly low-level daylight intruder missions over northern France, but as the Tomahawk lacked the performance for operations of this nature they were replaced by Mustang Mk Is in January 1942.

Below right: Close-up of two ground-crew examining the film cartridge of an F.24 camera. The camera housing hatch cover that had a circular hole cut in it for the camera lens has been removed, revealing some interesting detail.

13

Main image: At least two other Army Co-operation Tomahawk squadrons, 400 (RCAF), and 403 (RCAF), retained the black port wing marking beyond the Fighter Command 22nd April 1941 deadline for it to be removed. This was a special tactical marking for an Army (Southern Command) anti-invasion exercise, which was due to begin in late June, although by that time 403 Squadron was in the process of re-equipping with Spitfires. This photograph, thought to have been taken in April/May 1941, shows a trio of 403 Squadron (RCAF) Tomahawks, again two Mk IIAs, AH822 KH•R and AH896 KH•H, and a Mk I, AH878 KH•G, on a training flight.

Right: The subject of the illustration opposite, Mk IIA, AH822 KH•R, shows a rectangular-shape on the camera panel further back and lower (between the fuselage roundel and the individual aircraft letter) than the previous page's circular ports. Several other 403 Squadron Tomahawks feature this rectangular shape, as do some of 2 Squadron's aircraft (see p24).

Above right: Underside view of the trio showing that only AH822 KH•R then had the Night port wing and yellow-outlined roundel. Note that on the other two the port roundel is smaller, suggesting that the outer yellow ring was, or still is, there and that therefore these wings were also painted black at some point.

TOMAHAWK Mk IIA, AH882 KH•R, 403 SQUADRON RCAF BAGINTON, MARCH 1941

Modeller's notes

Aircraft
- Hawk 81A-2/P-40B.
- Barr & Stroud Mark II Reflector gunsight fitted.
- Ring and bead gunsight retained.
- Offset to starboard rearview mirror fitted.
- Aerial fitted on fuselage spine.
- 'Stepped' pitot on port wing.

Discussion points
- Rectangular-shaped camera port, (between the fuselage roundel and the individual aircraft letter), instead of the 'standard' circular port.
- There is still some uncertainty about the actual shades of the camouflage colours applied to Curtiss-built Tomahawks for the RAF. Some references quote DuPont shades which were produced to British MAP Colour Standards – Dark Earth 71-009 and 71-035, Dark Green 71-013 and Sky Gray 71-021, or, US Army Spec 3-1 shades, Rust Brown 34, Dark Green 30 and USN Aircraft Gray. Apparently Curtiss used whatever suitable paint shades were available, and sub-assemblies were painted before the entire aircraft was assembled so various shades could be found on the same airframe, as well as slightly mis-matched camouflage demarcations.

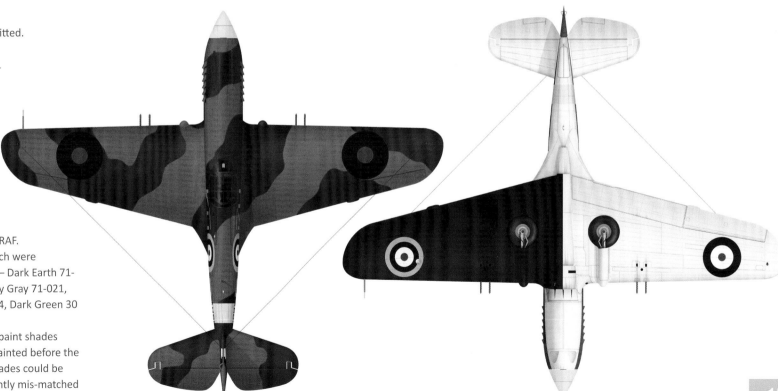

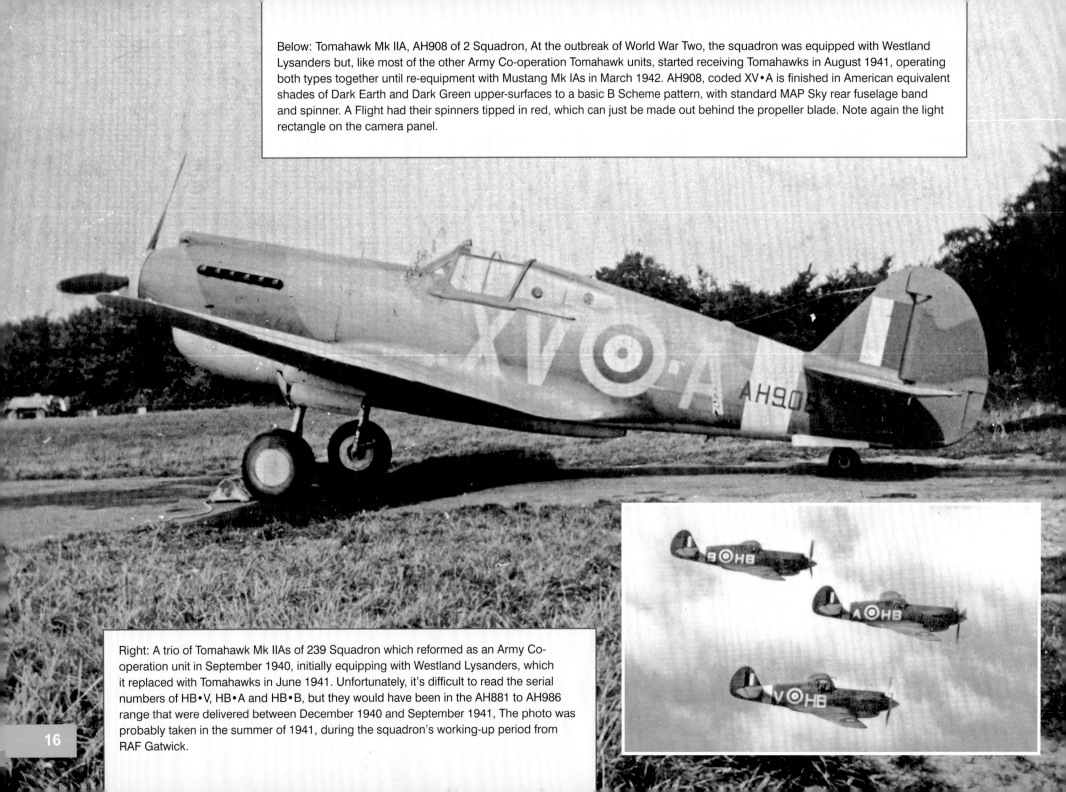

Below: Tomahawk Mk IIA, AH908 of 2 Squadron, At the outbreak of World War Two, the squadron was equipped with Westland Lysanders but, like most of the other Army Co-operation Tomahawk units, started receiving Tomahawks in August 1941, operating both types together until re-equipment with Mustang Mk IAs in March 1942. AH908, coded XV•A is finished in American equivalent shades of Dark Earth and Dark Green upper-surfaces to a basic B Scheme pattern, with standard MAP Sky rear fuselage band and spinner. A Flight had their spinners tipped in red, which can just be made out behind the propeller blade. Note again the light rectangle on the camera panel.

Right: A trio of Tomahawk Mk IIAs of 239 Squadron which reformed as an Army Co-operation unit in September 1940, initially equipping with Westland Lysanders, which it replaced with Tomahawks in June 1941. Unfortunately, it's difficult to read the serial numbers of HB•V, HB•A and HB•B, but they would have been in the AH881 to AH986 range that were delivered between December 1940 and September 1941, The photo was probably taken in the summer of 1941, during the squadron's working-up period from RAF Gatwick.

Above: Tomahawk Mk IIA, AH793 HB•Z of 239 Squadron, photographed at Gatwick circa July 1941.

The top photo shows to good effect the mid-fuselage hatch with the circular hole cut in it for the F.24 camera lens. The image under the cockpit canopy (inset) is a winged horse crop rather than the squadron's 'winged spur' badge, which commemorated 239 being the first squadron to work with an Armoured Division (in WWI), which included mechanised cavalry, represented by the spur.

Opposite page left: F/O Hollis 'Holly' H Hills in the cockpit of a Tomahawk Mk IIA of 414 Squadron, RCAF circa May 1942. Formed at Croydon on 12th August 1941, 414 Squadron (RCAF) was initially equipped with Lysanders but received Tomahawks the following month. The two types were used for training, the squadron not becoming fully operational until it had converted to the Mustang Mk IA. The 'Joker' card is presumably a personal motif. Of interest are the basic ring sight (A) and rear view mirror (B) both of which were offset to the right. The Barr & Stroud Reflector Mk II gunsight (C), which was fitted to RAF-operated Tomahawks upon delivery in the UK, has been swung to the left here. (D is presumably a camera aiming sight etched onto the canopy glazing. Note the thick internally mounted armoured windscreen (E).

Right: Pilots familiarising themselves with the instruments and controls of a 403 Squadron RCAF Tomahawk Mk IIA. Points of interest include the stencilling on the access panels just above the port wing root for the main fuel tank and reserve fuel tank, and the rear oil filler cap in the scalloped recess behind the cockpit with the access hole cut in to the glazing.

Main image: A formation of 414 Squadron RCAF Tomahawk Mk IIs including Mk IIBs AK185 RU•V and AK276 RU•F. Taken in early 1942, before the squadron re-equipped with Mustang Mk IAs, it shows the 6 inch wide yellow wing leading edge stripes from the outer machine gun barrel to 10 inches inboard of the wing tips, which was promulgated for Tomahawks with effect from 30th October 1941.

Left: Flt Lt F Bernard (centre) C/O of 1684 OTU Bomber Defence Training Flight, with his pilots in front of a ferociously marked Tomahawk Mk IIA. 1684 OTU moved to Little Horwood on 5th June 1943 undertaking simulated battles with Bomber Command aircraft using Tomahawk Mk IIAs.

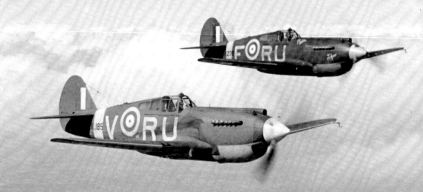

COCKPIT

Cockpit interior of a Hawk 81A-2/P-40B/Tomahawk Mk IIA. The inverted 'T-shaped' central instrument panel was designed to accommodate the breeches of the two .50 inch calibre machine guns over the cowling.

The instrument panel features the standard main flying dials. In the upper section – (left to right): Airspeed indicator, turn and slip indicator, rate of climb indicator; (left to right lower): Kollsman altimeter, turn indicator and slip ball, carburettor temperature.

Lower section (left to right): Fuel gauge, suction indicator, directional compass, manifold pressure, (bottom left to right) undercarriage and flap position indicator, temperature, oil pressure and fuel pressure triple gauge, RPM gauge and free air temperature.

On the left of the inverted 'T' panel is the Prestone anti-freeze warning switch, below which is the magneto switch.

The left side of the cockpit includes:-

A) Propeller control

B) Throttle quadrant

C) Mixture control

D) Rudder trim tab control

E) Elevator trim tab control

F) Fuel tank selector switch

G) An unusually positioned fuel gauge.

Curtiss was using DuPont 71-036 Cockpit Light Green, which had a pale pastel green/turquoise hue, for cockpit interiors at this time for the British Purchasing Commission Direct Purchase Tomahawks. The later Lend-Lease P-40 cockpit interiors were painted in the standard US Air Corps-approved green or yellow-tinted Zinc Chromate.

TOMAHAWKS IN THE DESERT

Tomahawk Mk IIB (Hawk 81A-3/P-40C)

A pair of Tomahawk Mk IIBs from one of the early delivery batches sent to North Africa, still in the Dark Green/Dark Earth upper surface Temperate Land Scheme. The Mk IIB was similar to the USAAC P-40C/H81-A3 and became the most common version of the Tomahawk in RAF service. Some 930 were ordered, of which 49 went to Russia, several were lost at sea during delivery, and most of the rest were delivered directly to RAF and Commonwealth squadrons. Fitted with improved self-sealing fuel tanks (introduced on this model), the American armament of four 0.30 inch calibre machine guns in the wings was retained together with the cowling top 0.50 inch guns, which meant that most of the Mk IIBs were sent to North Africa and the Middle East to avoid mixing them with the UK-based 0.303 inch Browning wing machine gun versions.

Uncrating Tomahawks at 107 Maintenance Unit, Kasfareet, (originally named Geneifa), in Egypt on the shores of the Great Bitter Lake beside the Suez Canal. Previously 'C' Squadron 103 MU, 107 MU was formed in December 1940 and quickly established itself as the leader in re-stocking fighter and bomber squadrons operating in the Western Desert. In total, some 4,500 aircraft passed through 107 MU during the war years.

Left: Delivery of Tomahawk Mk IIBs to North Africa in crates began in November/December 1940 and ended in August 1941.

Below: Uncrating the fuselage of a Mk IIB, which would then be mated to the mainplanes (above left) and empennage. Armament wasn't fitted for delivery, and the .50 inch machine gun fairings and carburettor intake have been suitably masked.

Once the airframe had been assembled, the armament was fitted and the engine tested.

Left: A fully assembled and armed Tomahawk Mk IIB, possibly already allocated to a squadron as it appears to have an individual aircraft code letter applied on the rear fuselage. It may also have had the Dark Green areas of the upper surface camouflage over-painted in a lighter brown shade, perhaps Light Earth or Mid Stone, as the light/dark areas of the standard B Scheme pattern are transposed.

Below: A Mk IIB, still in the delivery Temperate Land Scheme, having its guns tested. A close-up of the serial number appears to show it as being AK326, one of several airframes sent to Russia in September 1941. Note the removed panel in front of the windscreen over the fuselage-mounted .50 inch machine guns.

Inset: A fully assembled and armed early delivery Mk IIB still in the Temperate Land Scheme, taking off for either a test flight or maybe delivery to a squadron.

Main photo: Mk IIB, AK548, also in the Temperate Land Scheme, being refuelled from an Albion truck. Of note is the way the wing root fairing has obscured part of the fuselage roundel (also seen on the photo above). AK548 was allocated to 3 Squadron RAAF in July 1941 and flown during the Allied invasion of Syria. It was lost in August 1941 when it hit the ground low flying. Judging by the cordite staining under the wings the machine guns have been fired.

112 Squadron started re-equipping with Tomahawks in North Africa in June 1941. Its pilots soon adopted the now famous 'sharkmouth' markings on their aircraft's noses. It is thought to have originally been instigated by a Flg/Off Brunton, who painted 'shark's teeth' on his Tomahawk to distinguish it from the others at a distance, it is also thought that the idea was copied from similar markings on the noses of the Bf 110s of the Luftwaffe's II./ZG 76, the Haifischgruppe. Chris Wren, 'The Aeroplane's resident cartoonist had also illustrated the Tomahawk in the guise of a shark in his 'Oddentification' series – Number XIV which appeared in the June 1941 edition, which may also have suggested the idea to the pilots of 112 Sqn. Still finished in the Temperate Land Scheme, these two Tomahawk Mk IIBs which sport freshly applied 'sharkmouths', were photographed in the summer of 1941 probably at Sidi Haneish, Egypt. The aircraft in the background, AK461 'A', was shot down on 25th November 1941. The Tomahawk in the foreground, is thought to be AN218, coded 'B' which carried the name 'MENACE' in white capitals under the starboard cockpit sill and was regularly flown by Flt/Lt Neville 'Bowks' Bowker, DFC.

Below: 250 Squadron was the first RAF unit to re-equip with the Tomahawk in North Africa, in April 1941. This particular aircraft, AK374, LD•H, only served with 250 Squadron. On 26th August 1941, AK374 was being flown by Sgt Maurice Hards (who had just shot down a Bf 109 north of Sidi Barrani) when it was attacked by Fw Günther Steinhausen, a Luftwaffe 'Experte'. Hards made a forced landing, as seen here being inspected by RAF pilots. AK374 was repaired and eventually SoC in December 1942.

Right: Amongst the Commonwealth countries' squadrons to operate the Tomahawk, was 3 Squadron South African Air Force, which was equipped with a few Tomahawk Mk IIBs and Hurricane Mk Is between March and August 1942 when it was in Egypt. The rather battered state of the unit-applied Desert Scheme emphasises the harsh operating conditions during this period.

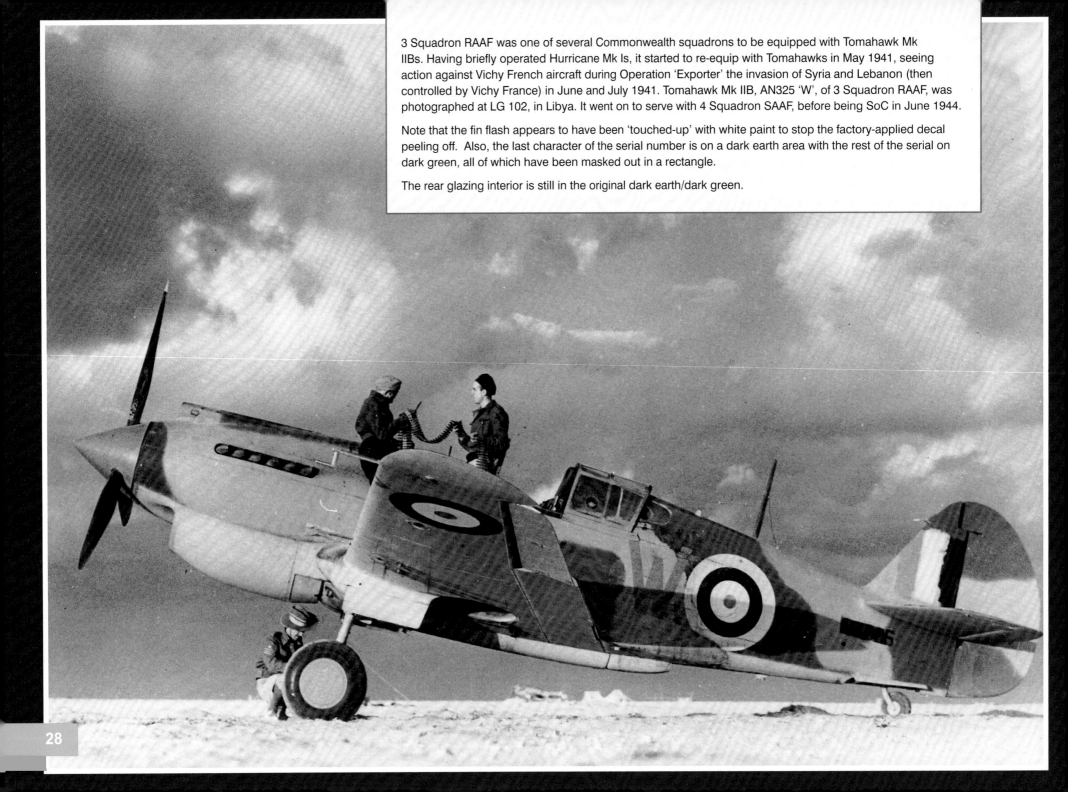

3 Squadron RAAF was one of several Commonwealth squadrons to be equipped with Tomahawk Mk IIBs. Having briefly operated Hurricane Mk Is, it started to re-equip with Tomahawks in May 1941, seeing action against Vichy French aircraft during Operation 'Exporter' the invasion of Syria and Lebanon (then controlled by Vichy France) in June and July 1941. Tomahawk Mk IIB, AN325 'W', of 3 Squadron RAAF, was photographed at LG 102, in Libya. It went on to serve with 4 Squadron SAAF, before being SoC in June 1944.

Note that the fin flash appears to have been 'touched-up' with white paint to stop the factory-applied decal peeling off. Also, the last character of the serial number is on a dark earth area with the rest of the serial on dark green, all of which have been masked out in a rectangle.

The rear glazing interior is still in the original dark earth/dark green.

TOMAHAWK Mk IIB, AN325 'W', 3 SQUADRON RAAF LIBYA JUNE/JULY 1941

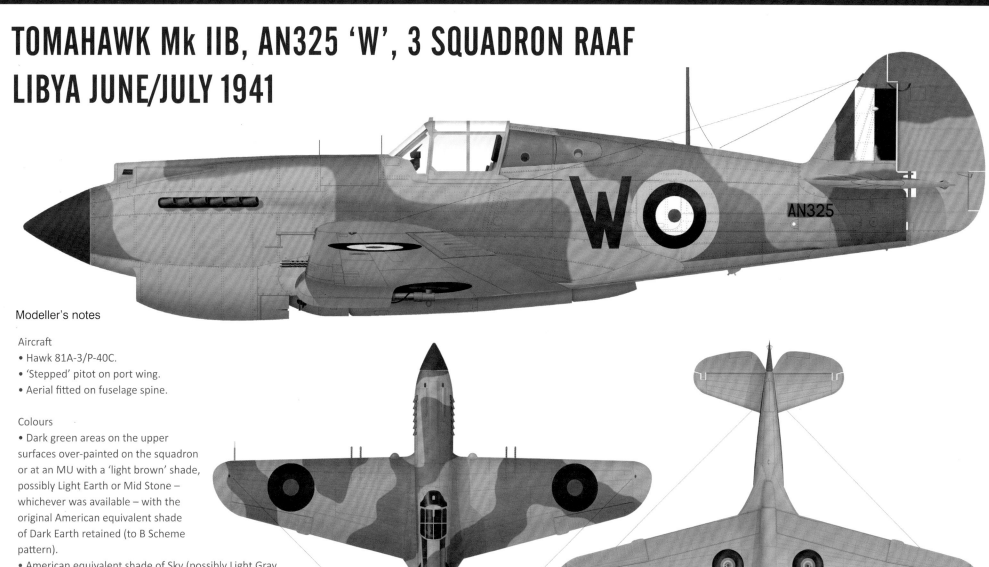

Modeller's notes

Aircraft
- Hawk 81A-3/P-40C.
- 'Stepped' pitot on port wing.
- Aerial fitted on fuselage spine.

Colours
- Dark green areas on the upper surfaces over-painted on the squadron or at an MU with a 'light brown' shade, possibly Light Earth or Mid Stone – whichever was available – with the original American equivalent shade of Dark Earth retained (to B Scheme pattern).
- American equivalent shade of Sky (possibly Light Gray 71-021, or Air Corps Bulletin 41, Light Blue 27) on the under surfaces.
- Red spinner and possibly red individual aircraft letter 'W'.
- Upper/under surface camouflage demarcation on nose along the engine cowling panel line.
- Standard pre-May 1942 style RAF roundels in Air Corps Bulletin 41, Insignia Red 45, Insignia White 46, Insignia Blue 47 and Identification Yellow 48, applied by Curtiss as decals during manufacture.
- The main-wheel hubs MIGHT be red too or still in the original Light Gray/Sky Grey colour.

Below: Tomahawk Mk IIB, AK475 GA•J of 112 Squadron undergoing an engine change in extremely primitive conditions 'somewhere in the desert' circa November/December 1941. The Tomahawk's Allison V-171-33, 1,090hp engine rarely lasted more than 60-80 flying hours due to the effect of the sand. The aircraft's lower cowling panels are in the foreground, with a very chipped 'shark-mouth'!

Inset left: An unidentified 112 Squadron Tomahawk Mk IIB, in unit (or MU) applied Desert Scheme with Light Earth or Mid Stone over the Dark Green areas and a full set of 'shark's teeth'! What appear to be yellow wing leading edges (applied outboard of the machine guns) were introduced on UK-based Tomahawks with effect from 30th October 1941, but were presumably adopted by North African-based Tomahawk units too, dating this photo to post-October 1941.

Close-up of the Tomahawk's cockpit area, revealing some interesting detail such as the canopy slide rail, internal bullet-proof windscreen with the Barr & Stroud Mark II reflector gunsight 'hidden' by the flying helmet. The pilot of 'Shirley III' is thought to be Lt R Pare of 5 Squadron SAAF, based at LG 121 Egypt in early 1942.

Inset: This particular Mk IIB, coded GL•S of 5 Squadron SAAF must have made a forced landing after May 1942 as it has the post-May 1942 style national markings applied. 5 Squadron SAAF re-formed as a fighter squadron in May 1941 operating from Zwartkop in South Africa equipped with Mohawk Mk IVs. It re-equipped with Tomahawk Mk IIBs when it deployed to Egypt in December 1941, and kept them until it received Kittyhawks in December 1942.

Left: A rare colour photo of a Tomahawk Mk IIB being serviced – possibly at Takoradi, Gold Coast (modern-day Ghana), West Africa. Takoradi was one of the main routes for Lend-Lease aircraft sent to British forces in Egypt and the Middle East known as the West African Reinforcement Route (WARR). Crated aircraft were shipped to Takoradi and assembled there and test flown, prior to being delivered to front-line units in Egypt in groups of six or so led by a bomber aircraft for navigation.

In this instance, the Dark Green areas have been over-painted in Mid Stone. The under-surfaces appear to be a shade of pale blue, possibly Azure Blue, although the main-wheel hub is a different shade, which might have been the American aircraft industry applied Light Blue 27. Also of interest are the exhaust manifolds fitted with flame damping fishtails.

Inset: A Tomahawk Mk IIB with temporary white paint applied by the MU at Takoradi to the rear fuselage and tailplanes as a hi-viz recognition feature in case the aircraft made a forced landing en route. Notice the Fairey Fulmar in the background, used for navigating the aircraft to their destinations.

THE FIRST KITTYHAWKS

Kittyhawk Mk I (P-40D) and Kittyhawk Mk IA (P-40E)

The first Kittyhawk Mk I (P-40D), AK571, photographed at the Curtiss-Wright Corporation's main production facility in Buffalo, New York. The main differences between the Kittyhawk Mk I and Tomahawk (inset) were the redesigned larger and further forward radiator chin air intake (A) and the removal of the cowling-top .50 inch guns (B). The P-40D also had additional armour around the engine and the cockpit. The engine was up-rated to a 1,240hp Allison V-1710-39 engine, giving better performance at altitude than the 1,090hp V-1710-33.

Left: The first Kittyhawk Mk I, AK571 undergoing flight testing in America. The RAF received twenty Kittyhawk Mk Is, (known as P-40Ds in the US), before an RAF request to increase fire-power to six .50 inch wing-mounted machine guns, resulted in the re-designation of subsequent deliveries of Kittyhawk Mk Is as Mk IAs (known as P-40Es in the US). AK571 went on to serve with 112 Squadron, but force-landed in the desert near Sollum, Egypt on 21st June 1942 and was abandoned.

Below: Head on view of AK571 awaiting the fitting of the wing mounted .50 inch machine guns. The distinctive redesigned and larger radiator chin air intake is made even more prominent in these views due to the higher upper/under surface camouflage demarcation and its lighter under surface paint shade which was peculiar to AK571.

At least six of the twenty Kittyhawk Mk Is produced for the RAF were shipped to and kept in the UK for various trials and evaluation purposes, including AK579, which underwent testing with the Aeroplane & Armament Experimental Establishment (A&AEE) and then the Empire Central Flying School (ECFS). Eventually ending up as a non-flying instructional airframe, 4099M, was used for ground training in August 1943. The aircraft is finished in the Temperate Land Scheme with post-May 1942 national markings, dating the photo to a period just before it became an instructional airframe.

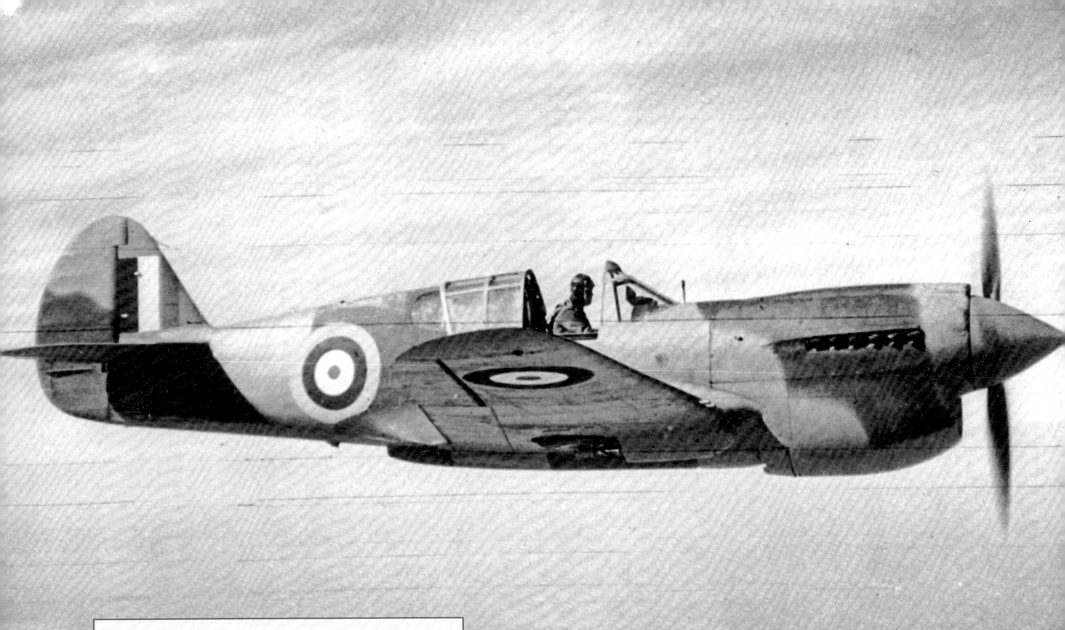

At least fourteen Kittyhawk Mk Is managed to make it to active service in North Africa, including his one, with the tailplane's shadow cast tantalisingly over the serial number. Deliveries of Kittyhawk Mk Is began in September 1941. At some point they were re-camouflaged in the Desert Scheme, as illustrated here, presumably by 107 MU at Kasfareet in Egypt judging by the correct application of the upper-surface pattern.

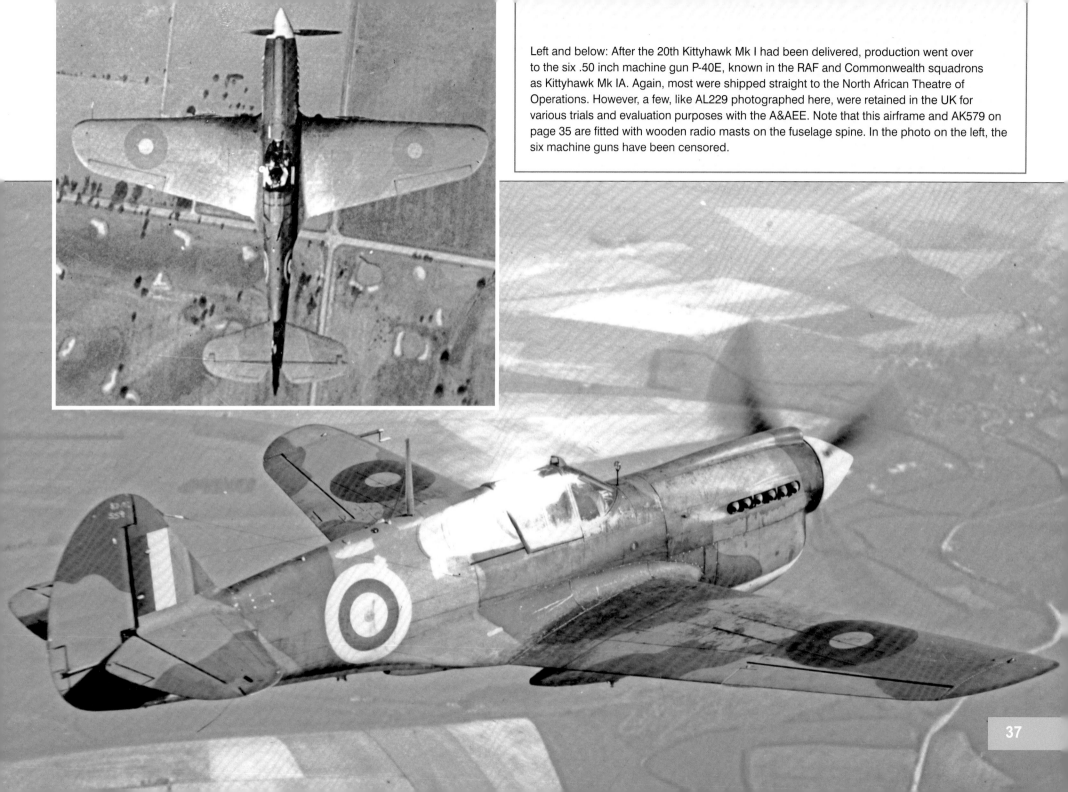

Left and below: After the 20th Kittyhawk Mk I had been delivered, production went over to the six .50 inch machine gun P-40E, known in the RAF and Commonwealth squadrons as Kittyhawk Mk IA. Again, most were shipped straight to the North African Theatre of Operations. However, a few, like AL229 photographed here, were retained in the UK for various trials and evaluation purposes with the A&AEE. Note that this airframe and AK579 on page 35 are fitted with wooden radio masts on the fuselage spine. In the photo on the left, the six machine guns have been censored.

Under-surface views of Kittyhawk Mk IA, AL229 undergoing trials with the A&AEE. The underside view shows to good effect the six .50 inch wing gun armament and the additional cartridge case ejection chutes in the access panels. The fairing (A) under the starboard wing near the undercarriage contains a G.45 camera gun installation. Also noticeable in this underside view are; the cockpit fresh-air intake (B) in the starboard wing root, an Identification Friend or Foe (IFF) light (C) under the starboard wing fillet, and a 52 US gallon centre-line mounted drop tank (D).

A classic shot of a 112 Squadron Kittyhawk Mk IA taxiing through rough terrain at Sidi Haneish, Egypt in April 1942, prior to another mission. The pilot is being guided by what looks like a fellow pilot sitting on the port wing-tip

Below: Kittyhawk Mk IA, ET265 GA•K of 112 Squadron still awaiting its 'shark-mouth' – or maybe not? ET265 appears to have only served with 112 Squadron for a few weeks, circa August 1942, and it is thought that this photo was taken at Landing Ground (LG) 213, also known as RAF Kabrit, a major RAF maintenance and servicing base used during the Desert Campaign. It is possible that ET265 is in the process of being refurbished, with new cowling panels (hence no 'shark-mouth) and rudder. This would account for the post-May 1942 fin flash being present with the pre-May 1942 style fuselage roundel.

Inset left: One of at least seven Kittyhawk Mk Is to serve operationally with 112 Squadron, AK578, GA•V, which does sport a 'shark-mouth'! A little more is known about AK578, which operated with 112 Squadron for over four months from January to April 1942. It was flown by Neville Duke, (the famous post-war test pilot), then a Pilot Officer. AK578 went on to serve with 4 Squadron and 5 Squadron SAAF, before going missing on a training flight while serving with 73 OTU at Abu Sueir (Egypt) in March 1943.

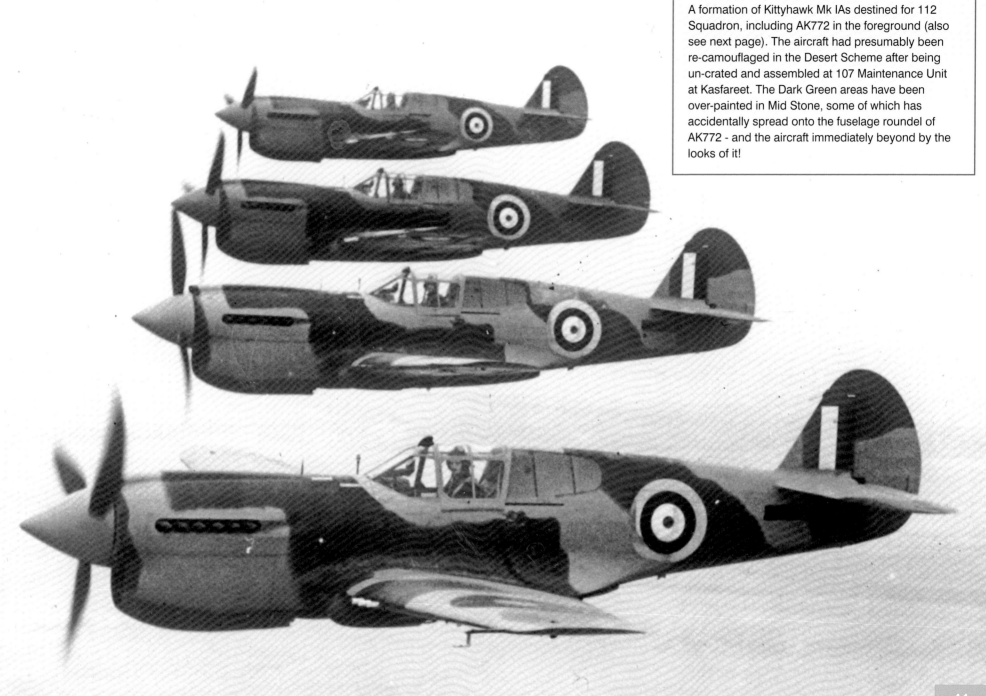

A formation of Kittyhawk Mk IAs destined for 112 Squadron, including AK772 in the foreground (also see next page). The aircraft had presumably been re-camouflaged in the Desert Scheme after being un-crated and assembled at 107 Maintenance Unit at Kasfareet. The Dark Green areas have been over-painted in Mid Stone, some of which has accidentally spread onto the fuselage roundel of AK772 - and the aircraft immediately beyond by the looks of it!

Kittyhawk Mk IA, AK772, (also seen on the previous page), now in 112 Squadron service with 'shark-mouth' nose and coded GA•Y. AK772 was taken on squadron charge in March 1942, but went 'missing' from a ground attack mission near Bir Hakeim on 30th May 1942. By this date, the squadron was armed with centreline-mounted 250lb General Purpose (GP) Mk 1 bombs. It will be noticed that this bomb is fitted with an extended nose probe, designed to make the bomb explode just above the soft sand for a better blast effect.

Just visible is the name 'London Pride' written in white above the 'Y'. Note again the paint over-spray on the fuselage roundel and the plugs in the exhaust manifolds to keep the sand out.

AK772 was flown by several notable pilots including the squadron's then CO, Sqn/Ldr Clive Caldwell when the squadron was based at Gambut Main, Libya, from February to June 1942.

Right inset: Armourers loading a 250lb GP bomb under the centreline of a Kittyhawk Mk IA.

KITTYHAWK Mk IA, AK772 GA•Y, 112 SQUADRON, LIBYA APRIL/MAY 1942

Modeller's notes

Aircraft
- Kittyhawk Mk IA/(P-40E).
- 'Stepped' pitot on port wing.
- Fitted with a centreline rack for a 250lb bomb.

Colours
- Re-camouflaged in the Desert Scheme by having its original dark green areas over-painted in Mid Stone, some of which had accidentally been sprayed over the port side fuselage roundel.
- Standard MAP B Scheme pattern.
- MU-applied Light Mediterranean Blue under surfaces.*
- Red spinner.
- White code letters.
- Standard RAF roundels and fin flash supplied by Curtiss as decals.

Discussion points
- *Under surfaces look very dark and MAY have been repainted in Light Mediterranean Blue at 107 MU prior to delivery to 112 Sqn, (Under surface colour applied after the Mid Stone).
- 6 inch high serial number is on an original dark green area which has been masked out in a rectangle.
- The rear glazing interior still in the original dark green.
- Main-wheel hubs in same red shade as the propeller spinner.

This page: Underside view of AK772, being fitted with a 250lb GP bomb, which was the usual warload for RAF and Commonwealth Kittyhawk Mk IAs. Again plugs are visible in the exhaust manifolds to keep the sand out.

As mentioned, the under surface colour does look very dark in this photo, and it is noticeable that it was applied after the 'Mid Stone'. It is thought that it had been painted Light Mediterranean Blue, or perhaps Azure Blue both of which photographed as quite dark shades with certain types of b&w orthochromatic film.

Other interesting points include the hydraulic brake pipes down the undercarriage legs, smooth tread main-wheel tyres, cockpit fresh air intake in the starboard wing root, open radiator cooling gills, fairly crudely painted teeth on the 'shark-mouth' and the well-worn propeller blade.

Inset: Another underside view of a Kittyhawk being 'bombed-up', this time with two 250lb GP bombs, mounted side-by-side, which was an unusual but not uncommon warload for RAF and Commonwealth Kittyhawk Mk IAs.

Facing page right: A wonderful colour shot of a 112 Squadron pilot standing proudly by the 'shark-mouth' nose of a Kittyhawk Mk IA. The identity of this pilot is a uncertain, but is believed to be Flt/Lt Costello, who returned to the squadron (having served with it when it flew Gladiators) for a few months in 1942.

Again the relative crudeness of the 'shark-mouth' application can be seen, and the under surface 'blue' appears to be very dark. Like AK772, it was probably Light Mediterranean Blue, which despite its prefix was quite a dark shade.

As Light Mediterranean Blue had been available from 1940 as a standard colour in MAP's Section 33B, and 107 MU was a major aircraft storage and equipment supply depot, it would have had access to the whole range of MAP paints.

Variations on a theme... No two of 112 Squadron 'shark-mouths' were exactly the same as all were individually applied, some more crudely than others.

Main image: A fairly crude 'shark-mouth' rendition on this Kittyhawk Mk IA. The under surfaces look much lighter than AK772's on the previous pages, possibly indicating the retention of the factory-applied, Light Blue 27, and the wing appears to have a yellow outer leading edge.

Right: Kittyhawk Mk IA, AK637, GA•F revving up at El Adem, Libya, circa January 1942. In this instance the 'shark-mouth' has lengthened incisors and a lot more teeth!

Main image: Kittyhawk Mk IA, thought to be ET919 GA•C of 112 Squadron taxiing through a typical sand cloud whipped up by the airscrew. ET919 has a relatively modest 'shark-mouth' and carries a 250lb GP bomb on the centreline.

Inset above: Kittyhawk Mk IA, ET790, GA•?, loaded with an American 250lb GP bomb under the fuselage. Flown by Sqn/Ldr Billy Drake, (who became the leading RAF P-40 'ace', with thirteen 'confirmed' and 'two' shared victories), he claimed his second 'kill' in this aircraft, a Bf 109F on 8th July 1942. ET790 was subsequently shot down on 22nd July on a ground attack mission while being flown by another pilot.

Kittyhawk Mk IA, AK593, GA•X of 112 Squadron, on its nose following an attempt to land in a dust storm on 27th January 1942 at Mechili, in Cyrenaica, Libya. AK593 must have only suffered superficial damage as it was returned to squadron service, only to be reported 'missing' from a bomber escort mission to Derna, in eastern Libya, on 8th February 1942. The open hatch on the fuselage side is where the desert survival rations were generally kept.

Inset: A 112 Squadron Kittyhawk Mk IA on fire, possibly following a strafing attack. Most of the fabric has burnt off the rudder and the propeller spinner looks a bit worse for wear!

Upper right: Kittyhawk Mk IA, AK688, OK•H of 450 Squadron RAAF, being serviced in the open (as was the norm) at one of the Landing Grounds between February and June 1942. Landing grounds included LG 139 Gambut Main and Gambut satellites LGs 142 and 143 in Libya. The squadron generally operated alongside 3 Squadron RAAF and 112 Squadron RAF, as part of 239 Wing, Desert Air Force (DAF), later known as the First Tactical Air Force. The squadrons' main roles comprised escorting daylight bomber raids and ground attack missions in support of the 8th Army. These were hazardous and resulted in heavy losses.

Lower right: Another squadron to receive Kittyhawk Mk IAs in early 1942 was 94, which replaced its Hurricane Mk IIbs in the February. Kittyhawk Mk IA, AK759, FZ•R was photographed in March 1942 during a short period of training following the squadron's first operational sortie with the Kittyhawk on 15th February. This was an attack on enemy positions at Martuba, Egypt, in which it lost four of the eight aircraft involved and its CO, Sqn/Ldr Ernest 'Imshi' Mason. Operations resumed on 20th March, under its new commanding officer, Sqn/Ldr Gordon Steege – this time with more success.

Photographs of FZ•R sometimes show it with red and white checks on the rudder, but in this shot the main item of note is the replacement 'dark' cowling panel under the exhausts. One of 94 Squadron's then new pilots was Canadian, Sgt James Francis 'Eddie' Edwards He became the third most successful Commonwealth Kittyhawk 'ace' achieving over a dozen victories in the type and also flew FZ•R on several occasions.

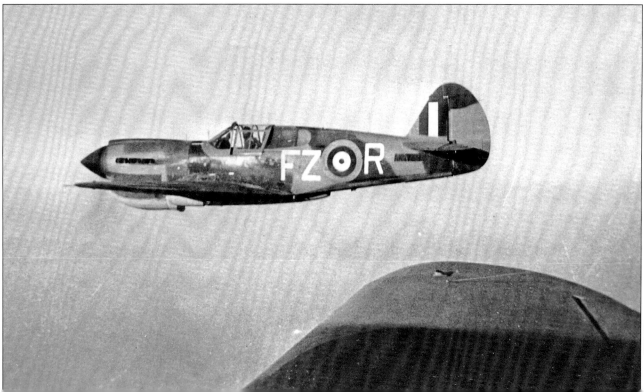

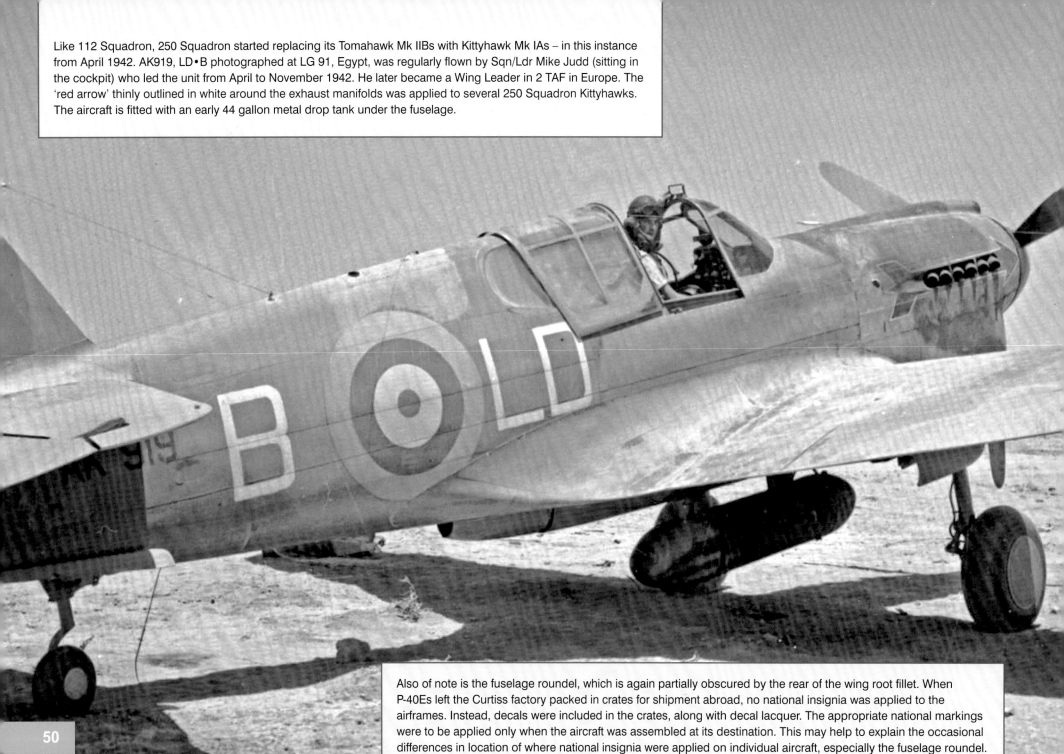

Like 112 Squadron, 250 Squadron started replacing its Tomahawk Mk IIBs with Kittyhawk Mk IAs – in this instance from April 1942. AK919, LD•B photographed at LG 91, Egypt, was regularly flown by Sqn/Ldr Mike Judd (sitting in the cockpit) who led the unit from April to November 1942. He later became a Wing Leader in 2 TAF in Europe. The 'red arrow' thinly outlined in white around the exhaust manifolds was applied to several 250 Squadron Kittyhawks. The aircraft is fitted with an early 44 gallon metal drop tank under the fuselage.

Also of note is the fuselage roundel, which is again partially obscured by the rear of the wing root fillet. When P-40Es left the Curtiss factory packed in crates for shipment abroad, no national insignia was applied to the airframes. Instead, decals were included in the crates, along with decal lacquer. The appropriate national markings were to be applied only when the aircraft was assembled at its destination. This may help to explain the occasional differences in location of where national insignia were applied on individual aircraft, especially the fuselage roundel.

Right: Two views of a Kittyhawk Mk IA in a 'dark' camouflage scheme, possibly Dark Earth and Dark Green, that maybe slipped through the MU's paint shop without having Mid Stone added. It may have been a later delivery airframe (possibly AL120) as it has post-May 1942 national markings. The individual aircraft code letter 'Q' would indicate it has been allocated to a squadron, possibly 5 Squadron SAAF.

Below: Another unidentified Kittyhawk Mk IA, taxiing with an American 500lb GP bomb under the fuselage, and again with post-May 1942 national markings. Camouflaged in the Desert Scheme with dark – (possibly Azure Blue or Light Mediterranean Blue) under surfaces, the 'last three' of the serial appears to be **793 which might be AK793. This initially served with 112 Squadron and was transferred to 450 Squadron RAAF, before being SoC in June 1942. Note the narrow yellow outer ring to the under-wing roundels. This was presumably added to make it stand out against the 'dark blue' under surfaces.

KITTYHAWK COCKPIT

The Kittyhawk Mk IA cockpit interior (thought to be AK753 of 94 Squadron) showing the starboard cockpit sidewall.

Lettered items include;

A) Canopy crank handle

B) Emergency hydraulic pump handle

C) Carburettor heat control

D) Control column

E) Basic instrument panel

F) Is a large electrical panel full of on/off switches and brightness dials for various lights and systems.

G) External gun sight, (offset to the right).

The gun sight appears to be an American S-8 Optical Gun Sight, nearly identical to the standard USAAF N-3A reflector gun sight, but made by the Star Machine Mfg Inc., New York, USA, to Air Ministry Specifications for fitting in American-made RAF-operated aeroplanes.

Kittyhawk Mk IAs were purchased under the Lend-Lease system, effectively being part of USAAF orders, and as such the cockpit interiors were painted in the standard US Air Corps-approved Zinc Chromate Green, often with the pilot's armour plate painted in Chromate Yellow.

Left: A 112 Squadron Kittyhawk Mk IA, with battle damage to the port wing (just in front of the aileron) the port tailplane, top of the rudder, and the starboard elevator. Once again the upper surfaces look 'dark' probably indicating a Dark Earth/Dark Green camouflage scheme.

Main image: Kittyhawk Mk IA, ET789, GA•C of 112 Squadron being inspected by ground-crew after force landing in the desert near El Daba, Egypt on 12th September 1942. The changeover to the new May 1942 style national markings had presumably been done 'on squadron' and in some haste, as the dimensions of the under-wing roundel aren't exactly 'standard'. ET789 had previously served with 450 Squadron RAAF. The upper surface camouflage is Dark Earth/Mid Stone in this instance.

MERLIN ENGINED KITTYHAWKS

Kittyhawk Mk II (P-40F) and Kittyhawk Mk IIA (P-40L)

As a solution to the P-40's poor high altitude performance, in June 1941 a USAAF P-40D, 40-360, was fitted with a British-built Rolls-Royce Merlin 28 engine with a single-stage two-speed supercharger. The Merlin did much to overcome the limitations imposed by the Allison, and an order was placed for 1,311 examples, powered by the American-made version of the Merlin built by the Packard Motor Car Company, under the designation P-40F.

The type was ordered for the RAF under Lend-Lease as the Kittyhawk Mk II, powered by a 1,300hp Packard Merlin V-1650-1. FL220 was the second production machine and was delivered to the UK for testing with the A&AEE in the summer of 1942.

The most noticeable feature of the Kittyhawk Mk II/P-40F – and all the Merlin-engined variants – was the absence of the long carburettor air scoop on the cowling top, which was no longer needed as air for the Merlin's carburettor was taken in through the re-designed chin intake, which also had a different radiator layout.

According to Curtiss documentation, all Kittyhawk Mk IIs (P-40Fs) delivered to the British between June and November 1942 were required to be camouflaged on the upper surfaces with "British brown on top of Army olive drab". 'British brown' was almost certainly a reference to Dark Earth while 'Army olive drab' was a reference to Bulletin 41 Dark Olive Drab 41 in lieu of Dark Green. The under surfaces were to have been 'Sky Type S Gray'.

FL220 was the second Kittyhawk Mk II to be produced and is seen here while undergoing trials with the A&AEE in the summer of 1942. It carries the post-May 1942 style national markings and a yellow 'P in a circle' prototype marking on the rear fuselage. It is possible that the under surfaces were also yellow to conform with the Camouflage Scheme for Prototypes as laid down in AMO A.664/42 of 2nd July 1942.

FL220 subsequently served with the Empire Central Flying School (ECFS) and Air Service Training (AST) before becoming Instructional Airframe 4103M.

Below: Short fuselage Kittyhawk Mk II, FL274, HS•V of 260 Squadron RAF, based at a Libyan airfield. Delivered in a Dark Earth/Dark Green upper-surface scheme, FL274 was re-camouflaged in the Desert Scheme by having its original dark green areas over-painted in Mid Stone. The 8 inch high serial number was masked out in a rectangle revealing the original dark green area underneath. The under surfaces appear to be in Azure Blue, again applied by the MU after assembly. The under-wing roundels have a thin yellow outline, which appears to have been introduced in early 1943 to make the marking more visible from the ground when employed in the close support role. The spinner is red and the codes are white.

Above: Line up of Kittyhawk Mk IIs, possibly awaiting allocation to a squadron. The upper-wing roundel on the aircraft in the foreground looks worn (as does the overall paint finish), so they MAY be awaiting disposal?

Left: Another line-up of unidentified Merlin-engined Kittyhawks, again either awaiting allocation to a squadron or disposal! Of interest are the two styles of exhaust manifolds on the front two aircraft; that in the foreground has circular exhausts, the one behind has 'fishtail' exhausts.

Below: The other Merlin-engined variant produced by Curtiss was the P-40L, a lightweight development of the P-40F, which confusingly was allocated the same Mk II designation by the RAF. The first fifty P-40Ls had the standard 'short' fuselage, but all subsequent airframes had the 'long' fuselage readily identified by the fin leading edge being level with the mid-chord of the tailplanes and the rear of the elevators being on a line with the rudder hinge. No long fuselage P-40Fs served with the RAF, all were standard 'short' fuselage variants under the Mk II designation. Armament was reduced to four .50 inch machine guns, (two per wing) although the three-gun cartridge case ejection slot panel was retained. The windscreen was re-designed, with a ventilation panel on the port side. (arrowed)

This particular Mk II/P-40L served with 3 Squadron RAAF, and was damaged at Cutella on the Adriatic coast of Italy, on 29th April 1944, when a USAAF Republic P-47 Thunderbolt pilot strafed the airfield.

Right: A close up of the 'long fuselage' extension showing how the fin leading edge is now well behind the leading edge of the tailplane.

KITTYHAWK Mk III
(P-40K & P-40M)

Main image: Three Kittyhawk Mark IIIs of 112 Squadron, preparing to depart from Medenine, Tunisia circa March/April 1943. The pilots of FR472 GA•L and FR440 GA•V, appear to be waiting for the pilot in the farthest aircraft to move out. The Mk III designation covered a mixed selection of P-40K and P-40M variants. FR440 and FR472 were P-40Ms all of which were produced with long fuselages to help counter the longitudinal stability problems experienced during take-offs and landings.

Inset: Another 112 Squadron Kittyhawk Mk III, (P-40K), coded GA•D, landing at Castel Benito, Tripoli, circa January/February 1943. As an alternative attempt to counter the longitudinal stability problems, some 800 P-40Ks (in the P-40K-1-CU and P-40K-5-CU production blocks) were produced with fin leading edge dorsal fillets (arrowed). This particular aircraft (a P-40K-1-CU) retained its US serial 42-45798, one of three 112 Squadron Mk IIIs/P-40Ks to do so, the other two being 42-45790 'B' and 42-45789.

Left: Two shots of another Kittyhawk Mk III with fin leading edge dorsal fillet. FR259 GA•X of 112 Squadron was 'damaged on ops' and force landed on 8th November 1942. The pilot, Flt/Sgt Randolph Smith RCAF, is standing with a member of 53 Repair and Salvage Unit (RSU) in the farthest photo. Incredibly, the aircraft was repaired and returned to service, serving with 250 Squadron, until it force landed after its engine failed on take-off in a minefield at Medenine, Tunisia, on 26th March 1943.

Main image: A Kittyhawk Mk III, with the P-40K fin leading edge dorsal fillet. Of the 600 P-40K-1-CUs and 200 P-40K-5-CUs that were produced with the 'short' fuselage and fin leading edge dorsal fillet, some 242 were delivered to the RAF. This particular example, FR338 GA•? only saw service with 112 Squadron and was eventually SoC in March 1946.

Line up of 260 Squadron Kittyhawk Mk IIIs at Castel Benito, Libya, in January 1943. Identifiable airframes in the line up include:

HS•X which retained its US serial 42-45798, applied to the rudder just above the level of the tailplane.

HS•B FR358 (see illustration opposite). Note the position of the rudder, offset to port, with the trim tab itself trimmed centre, making it look larger.

HS•V FR121 – (not to be confused with Kittyhawk Mk II, FL274, HS•V on page 65).

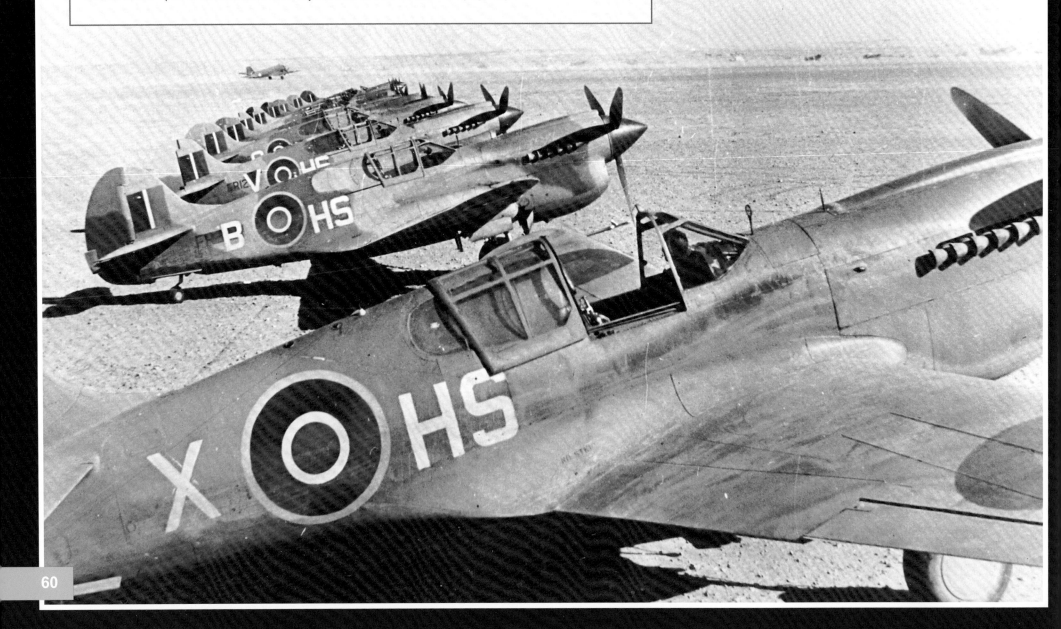

KITTYHAWK Mk III, FR358 HS•B, 260 SQUADRON, LIBYA JANUARY 1943

Modeller's notes

Aircraft
• Kittyhawk Mk III/(P-40K).
• 1,325hp Allison V-1710-73 engine.
• Fin leading edge dorsal fillet.
• 'Straight' pitot on port wing.
• 'Fishtail' exhaust manifolds.
• Centreline rack for fuel tank or bomb(s).

Colours
• Factory-applied Dark Earth/Mid Stone Desert Scheme.
• Standard B Scheme pattern.
• Azure Blue under surfaces.
• Red spinner.
• White code letters.
• Post-May 1942 style RAF roundels and fin flash.
• Thin Yellow outline to underwing roundels.

Discussion points
• 8 inch high serial number is on original dark green/dark earth area which has been masked out in a rectangle.

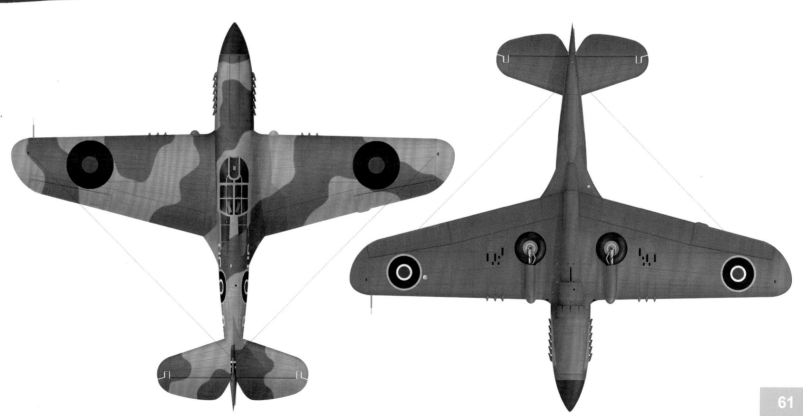

The same line up of 260 Squadron Kittyhawk Mk IIIs, as the previous page, but from a lower angle. FR358 HS•B is in the foreground, showing to advantage the shape of the fin leading edge dorsal fillet and the under-wing roundel with a thin yellow outline. Other points of interest include the 'fishtail' exhausts and the tape over the cartridge case ejection slots. FR358 went on to serve with 112 Squadron and was SoC in March 1945. Note the 500lb bomb in the foreground awaiting the fitting of the tail-cone and fins.

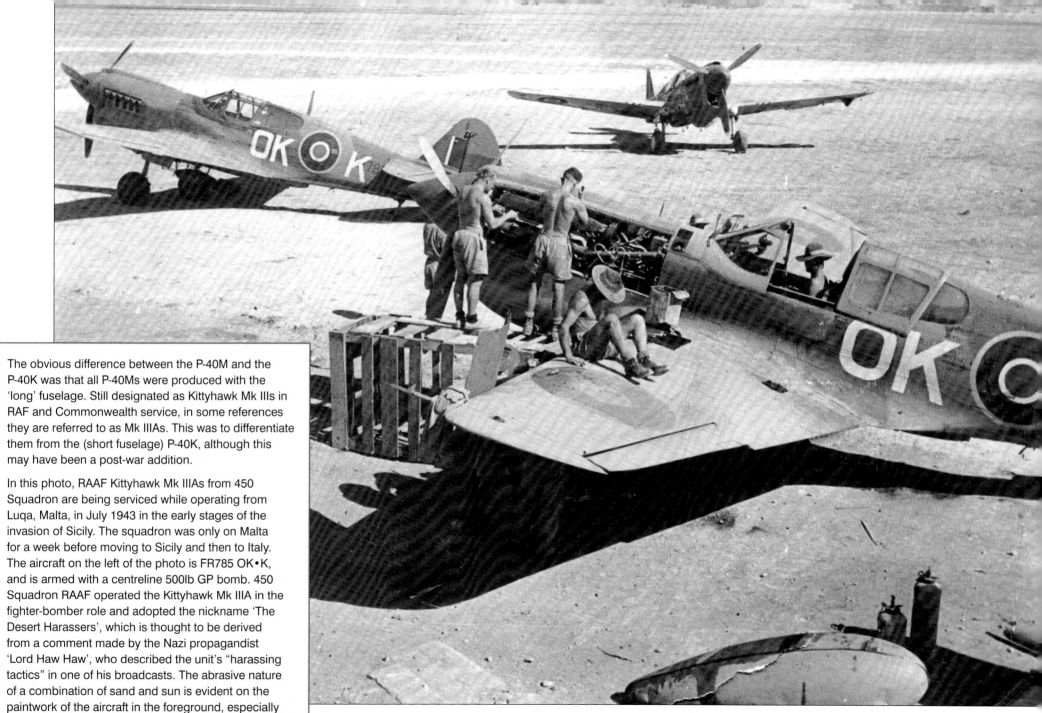

The obvious difference between the P-40M and the P-40K was that all P-40Ms were produced with the 'long' fuselage. Still designated as Kittyhawk Mk IIIs in RAF and Commonwealth service, in some references they are referred to as Mk IIIAs. This was to differentiate them from the (short fuselage) P-40K, although this may have been a post-war addition.

In this photo, RAAF Kittyhawk Mk IIIAs from 450 Squadron are being serviced while operating from Luqa, Malta, in July 1943 in the early stages of the invasion of Sicily. The squadron was only on Malta for a week before moving to Sicily and then to Italy. The aircraft on the left of the photo is FR785 OK•K, and is armed with a centreline 500lb GP bomb. 450 Squadron RAAF operated the Kittyhawk Mk IIIA in the fighter-bomber role and adopted the nickname 'The Desert Harassers', which is thought to be derived from a comment made by the Nazi propagandist 'Lord Haw Haw', who described the unit's "harassing tactics" in one of his broadcasts. The abrasive nature of a combination of sand and sun is evident on the paintwork of the aircraft in the foreground, especially on the upper-wing roundel. Also note the oil-stained 52 US gallon drop-tank, bottom right of the photo.

Main image: A 5 Squadron SAAF Kittyhawk Mk IIIA, FR817 GL•O, in Italy, autumn 1943, loaded with a centreline 52 US gallon drop tank. One of the main distinguishing features of the P-40M was the rectangular perforated grill air filter (arrowed) on either side of the cowling just behind the spinner, which allowed air to bypass the carburettor. This aircraft appears to have had its Mid Stone areas over-painted in Dark Green to provide better camouflage over the greener landscape of Italy.

The name 'Lady Godiva', appears under the windscreen, and 'a stork carrying a bomb' cartoon on the cowling side. The wings had full-span yellow leading edges and the fin had a white tip. The main-wheel hubs are thought to be in red and white quarters. Like FR781 overleaf, FR817 had very light under surfaces thought to be Light Blue 27 applied as part of the Curtiss factory Desert Scheme.

KITTYHAWK Mk IIIA, FR817 GL•O, 5 SQUADRON SAAF, ITALY AUTUMN 1943

Modeller's notes

Aircraft
• Kittyhawk Mk IIIA/(P-40M).
• Long fuselage.
• Quarterlight in the port side windscreen.
• 'Straight' pitot on port wing.
• Centreline rack for fuel tank or bomb(s).

Colours
• Dark Earth/Mid Stone Desert Scheme with the Mid Stone areas overpainted in Dark Green.
• Standard B Scheme.
• Curtiss factory-applied Light Blue 27 under surfaces.
• White tip to fin.
• Red and white quartered mainwheel hubs.
• Post-May 1942 style RAF roundels and fin flash with orange replacing the red.

Discussion points
• As the RAF and Commonwealth squadrons moved from the North African desert to the greener landscape of Italy, many units started applying Dark Green over the Mid Stone areas. Note how the Dark Green on the cowling side seems to have been painted slightly lower and the small area of US Mid-Stone on the chin intake.

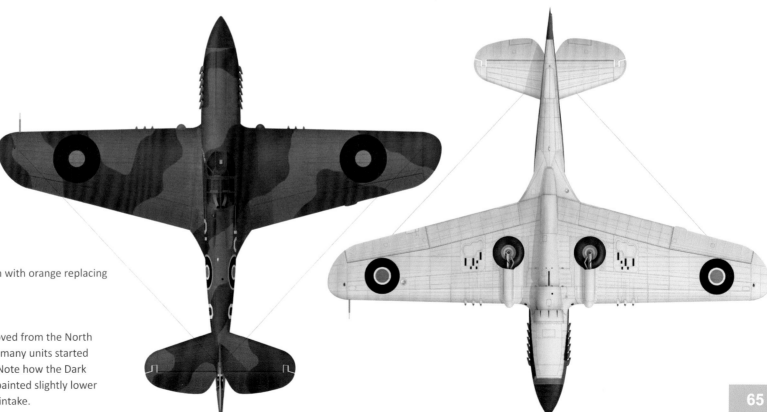

Main image: Another 5 Squadron SAAF Kittyhawk IIIA (P-40M), FR781 GL•H photographed at either Grottaglie, Bari or Foggia, Italy in the autumn of 1943. Again the P-40M's rectangular perforated grill air filter is noticeable, as are the 'fishtail' exhausts. This time the aircraft is loaded with a centreline mounted US 500lb GP bomb, with another on a loading trolley in the foreground. The name 'Raynor' is written under the windscreen and the disc with the white code letter 'H' on the undercarriage leading edge fairing appears to be red – a Flight colour perhaps.

Inset: A long-fuselage Kittyhawk Mk IIIA (P-40M) from 3 Squadron RAAF, photographed at Zuara, Tripolitania, Libya circa May-July 1943. Of interest are the five 7-point stars on the rudder (that may be pale blue) that represent the Southern Cross constellation seen on the Australian national 'Blue Ensign' flag.

KITTYHAWK Mk IV
(P-40N)

The P-40N was the final production model, which the RAF designated as Kittyhawk Mk IV. Featuring the lengthened rear fuselage, the most obvious recognition feature of the Mk IV was the cut-down rear fuselage decking behind the cockpit (arrowed) and extended perspex cover to improve rearward visibility. In an effort to reduce weight and improve the P-40N's climb rate, early production airframes reduced the wing armament to two .50 inch machine guns, but later production blocks from the P-40N-15-CU, including all those supplied to the RAF, reintroduced the six gun armament after complaints from operational units. The P-40N had magnesium main-wheel hubs to reduce weight and often the hub cap was off.

FX554 is a bit of a mystery. Although it is was one of 350 Kittyhawk Mk IVs delivered to the RAF between November 1943 and March 1944, and listed as being sent to the Mediterranean Theatre of Operations (MTO), it has a non-standard upper surface camouflage pattern and appears to have a European Theatre of Operations (ETO), Sky spinner and rear fuselage band.

KITTYHAWK MK. IV

Below: The later Marks of Kittyhawk could carry a heavy bomb load, especially on short operational sorties, as evidenced by this Kittyhawk Mk IV, FX745 OK•Y of 450 Sqn RAAF loaded with three British 500lb GP bombs, taxiing to the runway at Cervia, northern Italy, for a sortie in support of the 8th Army's spring offensive in the Po Valley. Again the dark upper surfaces are interesting and probably indicate a factory-applied Dark Earth/Mid Stone Desert Scheme with the Mid Stone areas overpainted in unit (or MU) applied Dark Green with Azure Blue or Light Blue under surfaces.

Left: A Kittyhawk Mk IV, thought to be a 112 Sqn machine, loaded with a US 1,000lb GP bomb under the fuselage and a couple of US 250lb bombs under the wings illustrating the variety of bomb loads the Kittyhawk could carry.

KITTYHAWK Mk IV, FX745 OK•Y, 450 SQUADRON RAAF NORTHERN ITALY, APRIL 1944

Modeller's notes

Aircraft
• Kittyhawk Mk IV/(P-40N).
• 1,360hp Allison V-1710-81/115 engine.
• Cut down rear fuselage decking with extended perspex cover.
• Quarterlight in the port side windscreen.
• Magnesium mainwheel hubs.
• Reduced diameter tyres from 30" to 27", (Mainwheel wells remained the same size as previous models).
• 'Straight' pitot on port wing.
• Centreline rack for fuel tank or bomb(s) plus wing racks for bombs.

Colours
• Dark Earth/Mid Stone Desert Scheme with the Mid Stone areas overpainted in unit (or MU) applied Dark Green, with Light Blue 27 under surfaces.
• Red spinner.
• White code letters.
• Post-May 1942 style RAF roundels and fin flash.

Discussion points
• Some late delivery P-40Ns were finished in factory-applied Dark Olive Drab 41 upper surfaces and Neutral Gray 43 undersides but FX745 is not thought to have been one of them.

Left: A 112 Squadron Kittyhawk Mk IV, taxiing for take-off loaded with a US 1,000lb GP bomb under the fuselage and two US 500lb GP bombs under the wings. What is not readily apparent is that the under-wing bomb racks were asymmetrically mounted – the rack under the starboard wing being fitted between the two outer machine gun ports, with the port wing rack fitted between the two inner machine gun ports.

Below left: A close-up of a 112 Squadron Mk IV, thought to be FX687 GA•K, also loaded with a US 1,000lb GP bomb under the fuselage and two US 500lb GP bombs under the wings. Beginning with the P-40N-20-CU production block, the under-wing bomb racks were cleared to carry bombs up to 500lbs.

Opposite page: The damaged tail of a 450 Squadron RAAF Kittyhawk Mk IV, FX529, which was flown back to base at Cervia, Italy, by Sqn/Ldr J C Doyle, the Squadron CO. It had been hit by anti-aircraft fire during a ground attack sortie over the 8th Army Front in early 1945. Note the wing root fillet has been removed, cutting the code letters in half.

71

Another 450 Squadron RAAF Kittyhawk Mk IV, bombed-up and ready to go! As with the photos on page 70, this aircraft is loaded with a US 1,000lb GP bomb under the fuselage and two US 500lb GP bombs under the wings. Other points of interest include the bomb rack sway braces, frameless canopy hood with deeper angled lower framework, Barr & Stroud Mark II reflector gun-sight and 'fishtail' exhausts.